Uncommon Common Sense

Practical Spirituality

Megan Wells

Living Food for the Soul

Copyright April 7, 2008 by Megan Wells

ISBN 978-0-9824472-2-2

Published by

Healthy Lifestyle Consulting, LLC

Just Give Me the Gist of It Books Series

Maui, Hawaii, 2007

To order additional copies visit: meganwellsbooks.com

Or call 808-244-0231

Or write Healthy Lifestyle Consulting, LLC

PO Box 511 Wailuku, HI. 96793

Printed in the USA. All rights reserved.

Cover by Vedic Design

Special thanks to Exper Giovanni Rubaltelli

For the Front Cover Graphic

"jmir1-103-4-fx" (c) 2008 by Exper Giovanni Rubaltelli (exper.3drecursions.com). Used with permission.

Introduction

Uncommon Common Sense

The Practical Spirituality of Uncommon Common Sense is a peeling away of the mysteries and complexities of advanced spiritual teachings giving you a glimpse of the simple essence behind them. Giving only the most necessary keys to unlock the doors to higher realization, these unique and revealing teachings use visions, modern day parables and simple examples to answer some of life's most perplexing spiritual questions.

Contents

Chapter 1

Swimming to Save Your Life

"The greatest happiness comes from feeling yourSelf grow spiritually" - MM

In my youth, I was perplexed about what it meant to really "contribute." At this time in my life, I had many people around me who, although perfectly capable of sustaining themselves, chose, instead, to live off of my efforts. I was struggling to understand whether ending their free ride would be an act of selfishness. One night, the answer came in the form of the following dream:

As it begins, I am riding in a small boat on the ocean with a dozen other people. The boat capsizes and sinks. I can see the shore, but we are a hundred yards out. I am the only one who can swim and all the people in the water are thrashing, in a panic, struggling to survive. I swim from person to person, pulling each one up out of the water and steadying him until he can breathe. As soon as each one catches a breath, I have to drop him and go to another person. I go from person to person, trying with all my strength to keep each one from drowning. There are so many; I feel intense panic. As I am trying to save them, I hear a loud voice commanding me to "swim away and save yourself." Thinking that would be too selfish, I ignore the voice. The voice gets louder. "Swim away and save yourself." Still I ignore it and continue. The voice becomes thunder and lightning. The authority of the command overwhelms me; it can only be God's voice.

I know without question I must obey. I literally drop the person I am holding up and swim as fast as I can toward shore. About twenty yards from safety, my heart is breaking. I have to look back to see what I fear will be an empty sea. Instead, I see what I never would have expected. I am given the perspective of a witness' seeing the entire event from the moment I choose to obey. My abrupt turning away and swimming towards shore shocks everyone; they stop panicking and become focused and calm. Studying what I am doing, they each learn to swim and are confidently heading to shore. To my joy, they are all saving themselves!

I awoke from the dream, feeling more awake than in my normal waking state. I had discovered something profound. To save myself and be an example of a whole person (a "holy person") is the greatest contribution I can make to others. It requires giving up approval, which is tied to (animal) survival instinct (see Chapter 4: The Crab Game). One person who has saved himself from the illusion of separation from God can save millions. "Being" the Divine Presence here and now is the ultimate gift anyone can give.

Chapter 2

The Velcro Theory: Our Need to Cling

"I am just a figment of God's imagination" - MM

One day, in my yoga practice, I became aware that I was "clinging" to my body. I also noticed I had the tendency to cling to all sorts of other things. What I mean by "cling" is: the tendency to want to hold on to people, situations, the way things are, my home. I asked God if I needed to work on ridding myself of this tendency and was surprised at the answer: "Yearning and desire are powerful assets when aimed at God." I was then shown a piece of Velcro with both sides stuck perfectly together and was told that the desire to cling was put into us intentionally by God so that we could cling to Him the same way the two sides of the Velcro are made for each other, created to form a perfect union.

Next, I was shown Velcro that had come apart, spinning in a clothes dryer. The side with prongs to attach became full of lint from the dryer and would no longer attach to the other side. God stated this is just what happens to us. He made us with a strong desire to cling to Him so we would be in steadfast union with Him. We became separated from Him and are tumbled around in the dryer of the world (living lives separated from God). We become attached to and filled up with the lint (material things) of the world. The *desire* to cling never goes away, even though our lives are full of everything to which we have attached ourselves.

We never experience perfect, seamless union with anything in the material world. Clinging to the things of this world was not what was intended in the creation of the clinging part of our nature, so material things can never be the perfect match our hearts all long for. Our desire to cling must be aimed totally at God for the fulfilling union to happen. Unfortunately, we are so full of worldly "lint" that we do not even possess our desire-clinging ability: the very thing required to have a whole experience of perfect union with God (our other half). We have to remove every piece of worldly lint to which we are clinging, to which we have attached ourselves, and with which we have satiated ourselves. We must cleanse our "desire nature" and aim our need to cling only at God. God is the only complete and satisfying answer. Cultivating the need to cling to God instead of trying to overcome the deep felt need to cling is the true answer to our hearts' longing.

Chapter 3

The Door to Heaven

"When all you want is divine experience, all you will have is divine experience" - MM

During one of my meditations, I was shown a Door to Heaven. The door was one that slides up to open, like a garage door. The door in the vision was the size of an ordinary front door to a house. One end of a cord was attached to a wooden bucket, the other to the door with a pulley in the center. The door was weighted in direct proportion to the weight of all my desires. All my desires had to be put into this bucket for the door to open. One drop of my desire not in the bucket provided insufficient weight to open the door.

It was clear, in the vision, that this was a mechanical fact, like a key fitting into a lock. When all the desires I am capable of gathering in myself are in the bucket of my desire to experience God's presence, the Door to Heaven automatically opens.

"Most people are splintered and need the glue of love to return them to oneness." - MM

Chapter 4

The Crab Game

"Only mans thought can block out the presence of God" - MM

After my morning meditations, I study nature. The most common show is the crabs that inhabit my beach. I watched one small crab working diligently to dig a hole for itself. Just when the small crab finished, a larger crab came and took the hole and chased the small crab away. I started complaining to God that I did not like the way He set things up on Earth. He then gave me a vision that forever answered my most troubling questions.

God showed me a crab that, I could tell, felt it had everything it ever wanted or needed. This little crab was fulfilled and content and felt blessed in every way. In this state of gratitude, the little crab felt overwhelmingly generous and wanted to share all it had with the rest of the crabs. The little crab announced to the other crabs on the beach that, having so much abundance, it just wanted to share its blessings with everyone. All the other crabs on the beach came running towards the little crab and tore its legs off, killed it and proceeded to fight each other and take everything in its hole.

I was shocked at this vision. God proceeded to explain that the crabs were doing what they were all programmed to do by Him. They were not being mean or evil or greedy; they were following the survival instinct He had created in them. They were, in a sense, being obedient to God's laws and plan. He then said, "Forgive them for they know not what they do." I was jolted with the truth behind what Jesus had said. This revelation of His understanding and wisdom was so different from what I had been taught and what is held commonly as the meaning behind His saying this. It was a statement of His compassion but even more than this; it was a statement of observation and truth.

Before this experience, I really believed that something was wrong with me. I seemed to attract exploiters into my life. From this vision, I saw that most humans function on a purely animal level. As they are not yet aware that they are spiritual beings, they exploit whenever, whatever and whoever they can, because, for them, it is a matter of survival, a matter of life and death. Like all lesser evolved creatures, they are programmed to stay alive at all costs.

God explained that there is another part of this vision that is important to understand. He programmed each species to destroy any deviation from itself. Any deformity or mutation in the wild is left to die or killed by members of the species, as a way of keeping the species healthy and strong, making sure the mutation or "different" animal does not reproduce and weaken the genetic line. From a purely animal, purely physical level, spiritual strength (i. e. compassion, generosity, consideration, selflessness) is perceived as a weakness to be preyed upon. Though Jesus was "different" in a good way, in spiritual terms, on an animal level, "different" is neither qualified nor analyzed. "Different" triggers the instinct to kill and eliminate.

Humans, on an animal survival level, react this way to anyone who is different, even if the difference is being more spiritually evolved. Millionaires, in the human animal world, are really only at the top of the "Crab Game." It's obvious that, if a person perfects the Crab Game, he will have recognition, acclaim and respect. If somebody evolves beyond the Crab Game, he will be disrespected, criticized and attacked because his presence challenges the Crab Game, all of its values, and all that people who play the Crab Game, embrace as their way of life. This is why Jesus said that if we become like him, we will be persecuted. Like Him, you *become* challenging and transformational energy.

Then, only those who want to transcend will value what and who you are. To the rest, you will bring out the animal instinct to prey upon you even as you pray for them.

Another lesson from the Crab Game is: no matter how big the hole or how much is in the hole, crabs are still crabs. The purpose of animal life is evolution: the survival of the fittest. The purpose of human life is spiritual evolution: to re-member, to re-connect with our true identity (which is spiritual). This is the purpose for which we were created. According to the Essenes, the original Christian teachings, man is not in harmony with life when he acts from infantile feelings after he is grown. In the same way, when man acts from animal instincts after he has become civilized, he is out of harmony with the law of life. When man is able to think his way out of danger, instead of fight or flee, but does not use his more advanced abilities, he behaves at less than his potential: like a bird, created to fly, hopping around on the ground. When man, created to be a spiritual being, behaves as an animal, he is not in harmony with his true nature and is not fulfilling his destiny. No matter how well he uses his skills and knowledge to get the biggest hole, he is still acting only as a crab.

Leaving the beach, that same morning, I saw the largest mounds, identifying the biggest crab holes on the beach. A wave came in and washed them all away in one second. Then I heard God say, "This is how all man's effort to amass material possessions, fame and power looks from My view. It's just that time, from human perspective, appears to be longer".

Are you just perfecting the Crab Game in your life or are you transcending it, to express the spiritual being you were created to be?

"Human animals respect you only if they fear you. If they feel safe with you, they don't respect you." - MM

"Gaining a profit is less important than becoming a prophet." - MM

Chapter 5

"Duality Supermarket"

"Desires are to the soul, what gravity is to the body" - MM

One day, while meditating, I had a vision. I was shown a store building with a large sign on the front of it: "Duality Supermarket." I entered the store and saw aisles and aisles of displays. Each item's description boasted, "This is all good and has no bad side to it." Even though each advertisement was for a different product, service, or experience, the advertisements all basically promised the same thing: only a good experience or outcome.

I selected something and was overjoyed to have what I believed to be all good. Of course, when I got home, I began to see that it had a down side, a bad side, a negative side. Outraged by the false advertisement, I took the item back to the store. The storekeeper was very cooperative and let me return the item for store credit. He said that I could shop around again and find something else more to my satisfaction.

I then found another item and the advertisement was impressive! It promised I would enjoy this item forever and it would never disappoint me. I was elated and took my newfound treasure home. After a short while, I found that this too was a false promise. Disappointed, I took it back to the store to complain about the betrayal I felt. Again, I was told I could return it and find something else more to my expectations.

Wandering around the store, I found the perfect thing. This time, the advertisement promised that it not only did it possess only a positive side but also that its benefit was guaranteed to last forever. I brought the item home and was ecstatic to have finally found what I had always been searching for: something that would bring me lasting enjoyment. After a brief celebration, the purchase no longer brought me enjoyment and, in fact, the sight of it caused me pain in the realization that, once again, I had been duped into believing the false advertising. I was angry and headed to the store to return the item. Upon entering the parking lot, I looked up at the sign in front of the store and was shocked. I had been looking for something that did not have any duality in a place that clearly stated that "Duality" was all that was available there.

"Duality Supermarket" is symbolic of the physical world. False advertisements are created by the master of deception. The Christians call this "author of false promises" Satan. In Eastern teachings, this illusion is called Maya. The advertisements are tailor-made for each individual who looks at them. They change to reflect each person's desires and cravings. Each advertisement promises only one side of duality. Duality is always inherent in the opposites of this world: dark and light, good and bad, up and down, in and out. Each carefully contrived advertisement also promises eternal benefit in a realm that <u>always</u> has a beginning and an end, a realm where nothing can ever last.

Enlightenment is simply realizing that joy that lasts cannot be found in a "duality supermarket" and being wise enough to see through all false promises. Meanwhile, people are on an endless "shopping trip" that always ends in pain, suffering and dis-"illusion"-ment. When this dis-"illusion"-ment becomes an awakening, one no longer shops at duality supermarket (the World) for what can never be found there. It is only in the spiritual realms, beyond the duality of the material world, that any thing that is all good and eternal can ever be found.

This endless seeking is a habit that needs to be broken to return to our natural state of contentment in the moment.

Remember the definition of insanity is doing the same thing over and over and expecting a different outcome.

Chapter 6

How Penguin!

"The mind once expanded can never go back to its original state" - WM

The last of my illusions about romantic love was shattered upon seeing the movie "March of the Penguins." In this movie, the penguins expressed the highest devotion and loyalty to the greatest extent possible. They demonstrated selflessness and commitment well beyond anything I have ever seen between humans, except on extremely rare occasions. What I realized was, that most of what humans call love is really only animal instinct.

Animals that survive by forming herds, or in the case of humans, tribes, instinctively know that if they are not accepted by the tribe or, even worse, if they are cast out of the tribe, it means death. All behaviors that do not originate from the awareness of soul identity, or, in other words, awareness that you are a soul, come from animal survival instinct. This instinct spurs a myriad of behaviors in humans. Everything about appearance, for instance, is selected for approval and acceptance by the herd (or to attract a mate, also animal instinct).

All the need for herd recognition is born out of the fear of not being accepted. All attempts to gain power and control in the world can also be traced to the survival instinct (having the most abundant feeding territory, so to speak). If you study all your behaviors, you may discover, looking honestly at their source, that they somehow come from animal instinct. Most humans fear public humiliation more than death because, on an unconscious level, it means certain ostracism from the herd.

The penguins huddle together in the freezing Arctic cold to survive. They take turns to be in the warmest center of the huddle and serve their time on the below-freezing outer edge, shielding those within from the bitter cold. If we saw this behavior in humans, we would award medals and consider it heroic. But when penguins do it, it is just survival instinct. Doesn't it come from unconscious programming that all must survive for any to survive? The male penguin shows such "love" and commitment in protecting the eggs while he starves for months waiting for females to return from gorging themselves on the plentiful food miles away. Nowhere in human behavior is more dedication consistently shown than this. Is it love that motivates him? Penguins do not choose this behavior; they are governed by it. It stems from the instinct instilled in them by the Creator to serve life by surviving. The following year, the penguins don't even recognize the mate they were willing to die for the previous season. Where did the devotion go?

I looked for any human behaviors not included in those demonstrated by the penguins and found only one that might be considered beyond animal instinct. That behavior is the wishing of spiritual enlightenment on another. In the book, The Road Less Traveled, the author, F. Scott Peck, defines real love as this wish and, based on the penguin's behavior, this is obviously true.

What we all commonly call love is animal instinct. The need for herd approval motivates even most churchgoers. A mother's "love" for her child and spouse can all be traced to instinct, as the penguins demonstrate so well. So, now, when I see noble behavior in animals, I have to refrain from saying how human they are and instead say how penguin! If this is what motivates most human behavior that we call love, ask yourself, have you ever felt anything beyond what the penguins demonstrate?

Humans are the only creatures that are cruel to each other. All the behavior in animals we may view as appearing cruel is only tied to survival, not vengeance and retaliation. Most cruel behavior in humans is tied to a "perceived" threat to survival. However, it is not usually a threat to the physical body, only to the false self-image. What is the false self self-image? Amrit Desai, founder of Kripalu Yoga (now Amrit Yoga) teaches that originally our survival instinct only applied to a threat to our physical form. We now consider any threat to our "self image" (what people think of us) dangerous. Of course, this threat triggers the same reactions as lions' attacking us. The fight or flight instinct is triggered and many defend their self-fabricated image as if their life depended on it, even displaying a ferocious killing instinct toward anyone who is perceived as the threat.

If ninety percent of our energy is used up in defending our false self image, imagine the tremendous contribution we could make to mankind not wasting our lives in this useless attempt to defend what does not even exist.

Chapter 7

The "I've Arrived" Practice

"Simple things are not so simple" - MM

Once I became aware of never being in the present moment, I observed that my thoughts were continually dwelling in some future time and place. I also discovered that I was not really living, but merely "intending" to live some day. This chronic habit seemed so ingrained that I saw I needed to actually retrain my way of thinking.

I began a practice to expose the lie that perpetuates this unconscious habit, which had robbed me of my peace. Through it, I discovered the root cause of this stubborn illusion that had choked out the experience of my real and satisfying life. In this practice, I would simply tell myself that the time I kept projecting myself to, had already arrived. I would simply imagine going to the time when everything I just had to do to be okay, content and at peace had finally been achieved. I let myself experience the feeling of having finally arrived. I would begin with a big sigh of relief: the way you feel when you overcome a big obstacle or make it to the top after a steep climb up a mountain. I would continue by concentrating on a state of gratitude, counting my blessings and what I had already done, experienced and obtained. This feeling of gratitude seemed to be very slippery and I needed to pay strict attention to it to hold on to it and extend the experience of it. I would repeat, out loud, the list of all I had to be grateful for and how relieved I was to have finally gotten to this far-off-in-the-distant-future place called "there."

A voice in my head began to interrupt this whole experience with the words "yes, but... " I questioned where this voice originated, that seemed absolutely intent on taking this state of contentment, rejoicing and peace away. And there it was: the ego, totally exposed and naked, hanging outside of all it formerly had been able to hide behind. This ego-voice had masqueraded as my protector and provider, always watching out for me. Through the "I've arrived" Practice, this illusion was stripped away, revealing the truth: that this ego-voice was actually the enemy that kept me from enjoying the peace and abundance I already had, but was continually missing.

Many times, I had to reaffirm that I had finally arrived at the made-up, fabricated, make-believe place that I might someday find or get to, where I would be content, fulfilled and at peace, a place where I would find enough of whatever it is that I think I am lacking. As many times as I affirmed this, a voice would interrupt with "yes, but... " and would begin to create a list of jobs needed to be done to some day get to where I already was: content.

The voice made up stories in an endless attempt to convince me. I could see that all these "what if" stories gave that ego-voice a job, something "it" needed to do in order for me to be okay. What a deceiver! I could see that this voice would always be spinning a yarn longer than I could reach, like continually laying out a railroad track for my train to follow, a track with no destination; its only purpose to perpetuate the endless trip. I realized that this had nothing to do with reality at all; it was all about job security for this ego-voice.

This is not the same as envisioning beauty and projects from a place of contentment, as an overflow from being at peace in the present moment or to set intentions to use your gifts and "contribute."

All this reminded me of a quote I once heard; "An American Indian chief pointed out that the white man was always in 'wanting.' This constant state of being driven by unfulfilled desires was seen as a spiritual 'dis-ease' to this wise chief." In our culture, it is accepted as normal because the disease is so widespread. Of course, it is a spiritual dis-ease. It causes us to be in a perpetual state of turmoil and torment.

Our physical necessities are important and, unless they are met, there will be anguish because these are real survival needs. But, all the ones that merely serve the false self-image are not necessary for us to survive. If you whittle down what you really need from what your ego voice wants, you will see there is very little that is actually "needed." Time to enjoy this small amount of what you actually need is really all that is lacking for contentment to be a way of life. In fact, time is the most valuable thing we have and almost everyone wishes for more time to enjoy life. Actually, it is priceless, since no amount of money can ever buy back time you have already spent or buy you more time in the future. Our real need is to develop our ability to appreciate what we already have to a greater and greater degree, not accumulate more things to appreciate.

Here is an antidote for the perpetrator of discontent in your head:

Happiness and contentment are found in using your time to enjoy what you already have, not in getting more of what you think you want, which always remains out of your reach.

Chapter 8

You are Not Your Toe

"If God is within us, what is self rejection?"- MM

Believing you are only your body, instead of knowing you are your soul, is like believing you are not your whole body, only your toe. If your toe made all your life decisions, based on only its own benefit, your life would be severely limited and the largest part of you would go unfulfilled. Of course, the remedy for this dilemma would not be to cut off your toe. Your toe is not a bad part of you, it is just a very limited expression of your whole self. Your toe can still have a life, it's just that the priorities of what is of value would change from what benefits only your toe, to what benefits your entire body, of which your toe is a part.

All the lesser or more limited aspects of your Self have a rightful place in your existence, once priorities and purposes are established. If all your aspects serve God, then all your limited parts have a purpose and a rightful place in your life. Each part or aspect serves the larger self, which is God.

This organization can be compared with a ship's captain and crew. When the crew takes over, there is mutiny. Each crewmember wants the ship to go where he can fulfill his separate desire at the expense of the rest on board, even at the expense of the survival of the vessel itself. There is war and chaos, as each crewmember tries to take control of the wheel. Only when a strong captain, who serves the best interest of all the crew and the ship, takes charge, can there be peace. Only then, can all the energies of the crew be a cohesive force, working for every member's benefit. Only then, can the ship actually sail.

Without the guidance of a vaster perspective, the energy of the crew dissipates into struggle.

This is how we limit ourselves when we forget we are more than a physical body; when we forget we are a spiritual being. Can you imagine believing that what your toe needs is all you need because you are no more than your toe? What if you allowed your toe's needs to govern your life and were dragged around by your toe to get only its needs met? We all know we are more than that. We merely ***have*** a toe, we are not our toes.

In the same way, we are governed by not only our physical needs, but mostly ego-mind needs, and have forgotten that we are actually spiritual beings. Many religious teachings stress that we must overcome, suppress or get rid of our lower nature to ascend spiritually, but that would be like cutting off your toe to deal with what is only really a problem with identity and priorities. The Creator made us with many qualities and instincts; none is a mistake. All are useful when they fulfill the purpose for which they were created: to serve the greater Self or God.

Our ambition, and even aggression, can be focused to serving God. It is stifling of our power to try to suppress or cut off any part of our nature, even the lower animal nature. When the soul is the captain of the ship, the boss, the authority and guiding identity, everything and everyone that makes up who we are falls in line, like the planets, all in their proper orbit, spinning perfectly, always in alignment with the true purpose for which they were created. They then work as a whole expression to serve God and the greater Self of mankind.

Many men and women have qualities that they have been taught are flaws by religious thinking. They struggle to overcome them instead of redirecting these aspects of themselves, by giving them a job to keep them out of trouble, so to speak. All our qualities become Divine when used for the Divine Purpose of spiritual evolution and reunion with our true Self, the Creator Himself. When the toe directs the body, instead of the body's directing the toe, then even the toe feels limitation, bondage and confinement to a limited self with a limited purpose. When the body directs the toe, there is a feeling of liberation, instead of confinement, for both the toe and the body.

End your internal war and bring peace within yourself once and for all by taking a stand about who will guide the ship of your life. For the sake of all on board, make a firm vow now that all else will submit to being guided by the Soul captain of your ship.

Chapter 9

Satiation: The Ego's Lie about Fulfillment

"The ego wants a permanent state of temporary pleasure" - MM

We medicate ourselves to avoid feeling pain. For most people, it is emotional pain and beneath that is always the spiritual pain of separation from your true Mother and Father-- God.

What is "medicating?" It is decreasing our sensitivity by saturating (to fill so that no more can be added). The saturation is a form of numbing. Our sensitivity is what enables us to feel or sense God. We cannot know God by thinking of Him, for by design we can only think of something from which we are separate. To know or experience God is to *feel* God. When we saturate or dose ourselves with sensual experience, food, sex, alcohol or drugs, we numb ourselves. It is no different from taking a pain-killing drug. We are then incapable of tuning in with all our sensitivity to Divine Presence. We no longer have access to feeling God, since we no longer have access to our sensitivity, which is, in reality, our receptivity. "Medicating" is trading the feeling of connection to Source for a state of nothingness. But, with a relief of pain, stress or frustration, we accept this temporary solution in place of the healing Presence of God.

Experiencing the Presence of God is a fulfilling, more aware, more sensitive, state of being; one where expansion and spiritual evolution are so nourishing that the pain, anxiety and stress just drop away like light filling a dark room; true healing is then experienced. Satiation is merely treating a symptom, providing a temporary suppression. For life-changing healing, we must allow ourselves full sensitivity and courageously face the message of pain that signals the need for healing, instead of running from it. Confronting what we need to heal is the only way to lasting happiness but confronting pain requires us to overcome animal instinct which tells us to escape and run from it.

The numbing experience, by sensual satiation, is a maddening one. The pain, stress, or anxiety still awaits emergence, the very moment the satiation wears off. Since sensual satiation is a part of duality, it has a beginning and an end. In fact, the moment satiation is attained, it begins to diminish, as does all temporary experience in the physical world of duality.

Longing in the heart, felt by a person disconnected from his or her own God-Self, seeks fulfillment with human love. This feeling of emptiness is caused by separation from the God-self. Because the separation is part of the world of duality, it can only be sustained by continual effort and the imperfection that accompanies this "almost" fulfilling "love" state causes anxiety along with the feeling of contentment. So, it is not truly a feeling of contentment, which, by definition is a constant state, not an impermanent one.

Once we are capable of seeing that a permanent state in the outer world is unattainable, the truth is realized. All longing, need and desire can be actually *cultivated* and focused to Divine experience. The more focused and awake longing becomes, the more permanent the state of oneness, bringing an end to all suffering. As in all attempts to treat symptoms, not only is precious time lost that could be used for true healing, but also the ability to address the real cause of suffering is diminished. For instance, medicating, numbing and suppressing the cells of the body may lesson pain, but it also paralyzes the cells' natural ability to heal. To heal, they need to be enlivened, awakened and sensitized (just the way you need to be wide awake to efficiently carry out your work).

There is an unconscious accepted myth that the body does not want to heal, revealing the truth that every cell in the body is programmed to do nothing else but carry out all the forms of healing, and that our interference in their inborn agenda is what causes us so much suffering. Much like a plant that wants to grow, bloom and bear fruit, our body always wants to heal and perfect itself. It has an inborn desire to become all it is capable of, which is actually unlimited. In the same way our glands secrete hormones that change us from infant to toddler to child to adolescent and then adult, our body is capable of one further change from human animal to the spiritual human.

Temporary satiation or permanent liberation: you must choose. You must choose to want God at all costs. Be willing to die for your cause and you will be born into eternal existence, the dominion you were created to inhabit. When all craving stops, clear vision of reality is born, untainted with interference by the mind (I. e. "This is good because I want it"). Fasting heightens the longing and sensitizes the hunger for something more spiritual. It is actually spiritual medicine. That is why Christ taught this by example as a path to liberation and enlightenment. It is unfortunate that the art of purification and it's relevance to awakening has been lost and completely eliminated from Christ's teachings except in the Essene teachings which are original unaltered Christian scriptures. (See Essene Gospel of Peace by Edmond Szekely). *

For guidance on the path of physical purification and healing read Don't Pollute Your Own Stream by same author

Chapter 10

The Discounter

"Fear is faith in what Satan says" - MM

After having multiple experiences of the Divine presence manifesting in my outer life, I became aware of a voice that seemed to be purposely discounting the experiences. I had been told that I had an unusual astrological configuration, opposite to the norm. A Tibetan lama, who did my chart, said that my ego told me I was less than I really am (as opposed to common egos which make a person think the ego is more than it really is).

An example helped me see what an average ego looks like from a detached perspective. I was shown a page of pixels (dots) covering it. Each pixel made up one tiny part of the picture. Together, the pixels made one whole image. Then, I was shown one pixel, who believed that all the other pixels revolved around it, were only there for its benefit, for no other purpose than to serve it. This was an example of an egotistical viewpoint. Of course, you can see that this is not true for the pixel in a picture or for any human being. We are all just part of a larger whole. Our purpose is to play our part and be a part of the bigger purpose/picture for which we were created; to be our unique Self and be in harmony with the bigger picture, the bigger purpose, the purpose that serves the entire picture.

Back to the discounter…I began to question what possibly could motivate this voice. It always served to keep my awareness from celebrating the truth that I had been, and am, blessed by God. I see this voice as the ego's attempt to preserve its life, which crowds out the true experience of knowing yourself as a soul, one with God and fulfilled.

This voice masqueraded in my life as protecting me from pride. What became clear was that pride is something that belongs to the false self-image. Pride is really the inferiority of the false self. The soul does not need this to offset any lack. The soul knows it is perfect and enough. Discounting the joys of spiritual experience only serves the ego, and again guarantees job security for it in its endless attempt to be "enough" and valuable. Of course, it can never be enough because it is only a figment of its own imagination.

Our soul is a figment of God's imagination. Being God's creation, we are perfect, whole and complete. Looking at God's creation, we can know that all of God's creation is perfect, whole and complete. Now, when I hear that voice, I just tell it to shut up! You must be abrupt about it. This silver-tongued devil, literally, will talk you out of who you really are, your Soul, every time, if you listen for even a second. Can you make a flower more perfect? A good affirmation for this is "I am a figment of God's imagination."

Can you make a flower more perfect?

One of the best examples of determining what to accept among voices in your head was seen in a children's seminar that I attended. A large cardboard box was turned upside down with a door cut in it. The children took turns going inside the box alone. The rest of the children lined up and one by one knocked on the door of the box. The child inside was instructed to ask, "Who's there?" The child at the door would answer with either a life-affirming response or a negative one. "You are powerful," a child would answer. The child in the box would then invite the child into the box to be with him. The next child would knock on the door and the child in the box would ask, "Who is there?" and the child would answer, "You are stupid." The child in the box would command, "Go away; I am not letting you in." The box was symbolic of the mind and the children at the door were thoughts. In this exercise, the children were taught to discern life-affirming thoughts from self-defeating, limited programming; negative thoughts from others and their own mind. If you engage in any form of inquiry with any detail of a negative thought, you have brought them into the "box" of your mind. Just don't open the door of your mind at all and say, "Go away!"

Chapter 11

Touching God:
Nature is God's Physical Form

"I have an open account with the infinite source" - MM

It is just as absurd to deny that your soul comes from God, the Father, as it is to try to deny that your physical body comes from your blood father's seed. I began to experience this body as merely dust, water and air, which is arranged and held together in a unique way by Mother Nature. Visualizing this, I came face to face with the inability of my limited mind to do such an insurmountable thing as to form life out of dust and animate it. No possibility can exist other than that of Divine Mother Nature doing this. Then the certainty that Divine Mother Nature is truly my mother, the mother of this body, wipes away any illusion of separateness.

When you ask where your spirit comes from the question will take you to the only answer possible as well. Ask yourself, "Where does my soul come from?" There is only one possibility and in that answer lies a reunion with the Father. He really is the Father of our souls. Affirmations can help heal the illusion of separation:

You truly are my Father. I am safe in my Father's house. I am healed in the temple of Thy presence.

I am in my Mother (nature) and she is in me. Mother natures' body is my body and my body is Mother Natures' body. I and my Mother are one.

I am in my Heavenly Father and He is in me. My spirit is Your spirit; Your spirit is my spirit. I and my Father are one.

Chapter 12

Making God in your Parents' Image

"Remember… ignorant is derived from ignore" - MM

At one point, I had to admit that I didn't trust God and when I really searched my soul, I realized that it was because my concept of God was flawed. As a child, I considered my parents to be God: I was completely dependant on them for everything. My parents provided all of my sustenance from the womb on: food, shelter; took care of all my needs and protected me. They did this imperfectly. I would cry and they wouldn't come or I would be hungry and wouldn't be fed. So, I began to not trust them.

As I grew up, I became more and more intolerant of my parents' frailties and limitations because I was expecting them to be God and, on the other side of this faulty logic, I was making God in their image. I had no concept of what God is. I carried this mistake to its extreme when I actually felt the same way toward God as I felt toward my parents. When I realized all of this and restructured my thinking toward my parents (that they were imperfect human beings doing the best they could). I realized that they weren't God, and therefore could not possibly be omnipresent, omnipotent, all giving, all powerful, all protecting, all knowing, as I so longed for them to be as a child. When I let go of my infantile expectations of them I could actually forgive my parents and love them regardless of what they did or didn't do while bringing me up and caring for me.

The big benefit was that I redesigned my concept of God. I realized that God is infallible, is omnipresent, is omnipotent and will not let me down. I can rely upon this real God. I learned to trust God when I no longer made Him in my parents' image.

Chapter 13

A Rock in the Stream

*"You can't solve problems with the
same mind that created them" - MM*

My friend and respected teacher, Yogi Amrit Desai (AKA Gurudev), had a break between flights leaving Maui, so I offered to take him to see Iao Valley's beautiful jungle rivers.

I marveled at how he spontaneously rolled up his pant legs and waded out into the stream, even though he was impeccably dressed to get on a plane. As he literally merged into the stream, there was such delight on his face. He glowed like an ecstatic three-year-old child and was fascinating to watch. Whenever I am near him, I study him because he is the eighth wonder of the world. He is unlike any other creation because he is an expression of Unity Consciousness and oneness. He appears different from other human beings because he expresses such freedom and effortlessness in his life. His grace is a state so inspiring and attractive that it is hard to take your eyes off of him when you are in his presence. I was intently watching him frolic in the stream and I recognized that Gurudev is like a stream. His presence is like the water that effortlessly flows. Even if there is a rock in the stream, this water known as Gurudev just flows around it and continues without any effort, reaction, disturbance or resistance.

I acknowledged the difference between how Gurudev was flowing through his life (which literally is a flow) and how I was traversing through mine. I became aware, that day, that if I am the water (my life) and there is a rock in my stream (a perceived obstacle), I stop at the rock, remark that there is a rock in the way of my water flowing and become literally attached to the rock while I try to identify it. I saw a vision of myself with my arms around the rock holding on to it while I analyzed it. How big is the rock? What kind of rock is it? Why is the rock there? When did the rock get there? I had the tendency to form a relationship with the rocks in my stream. I would unconsciously create a relationship with any obstacle that came before me. What I saw demonstrated that day by Gurudev was his mastery of life, reflected in his ability to flow past all obstacles and not create any relationship with them. He just *flows* through life, literally like water in a stream. It was quite a lesson for me to learn to not be attached to circumstances being my way.

By watching him that day, I saw clearly, by comparison, that I habitually became involved with every obstacle. The mirror of his clear reflection illuminated my own efforts to manipulate life to unfold in a way that I believed would fulfill my desires. Gurudev's freedom to flow through life came from the fact that he was no longer trying to manipulate life to fulfill any desires: he had no unfulfilled desires. He was obviously in a state of fulfillment, self-contained and no longer driven by any desires. This state of fulfillment released him from the need to manipulate circumstances or to make them any different from the way they are unfolding around him. He no longer needs to try to change reality in an unrealistic way.

You can't change reality anyway but the rest of us seem to waste a lot of time and energy trying. Gurudev merely accepts reality as it unfolds before him. He is just a happy witness to it all. This is what gives him the beautiful quality of a stream, effortlessly flowing around all the rocks in his way. He is a living version of the song: "row, row, row, your boat gently down the stream, merrily, merrily, merrily, merrily, life is but a dream…"

Chapter 14

Perfect Infant Self: Trying on Identity Outfits

"I am not a human having a spiritual experience; I am a spirit having a human experience." - MM

At the time of our birth, we are perfect creations. Regardless of how a newborn looks or the state of its health, it is, at the moment it first arrives, the greatest undistorted expression of its true Self (that which it was created to be). This brand new human being has not yet identified with the changing material world. The infant human is like a perfect musical note coming from a musician with perfect pitch (God), not yet having passed through a distorted amplifier (the man-made world). At the moment of birth, the human being is not man-made, he is God-made. This God-made creation becomes a man-made creation by identification with the physical environment, in a process of covering over the Perfect Infant Self.

Aside from survival needs, which cause discomfort, a baby is its own source of joy. It experiences its own soul (which is bliss) as the entirety of itself. It floats in and out of its body, not yet identified with the limitation of human form. This sense of freedom is a joy in itself. The infant is identified only with its immortal spirit, which possesses unlimited potential.

Soon after birth, the soul becomes identified as being limited to its physical form. The first identity layer is "I am a human in this physical body" rather than the truth: "I am an immortal spirit." The next layer begins when the baby is told "You are beautiful." It is identified as some "thing," as opposed to being everything. This programming is the origin of identification with duality. If nothing were considered ugly, there would be nothing with which to compare beauty; beautiful and ugly exist only in duality. Next arise questions and self-judgment: "What if I am no longer beautiful? Is my brother more beautiful?" What was intended to be a positive statement toward the baby becomes a limiting one, teaching this immortal, unlimited soul, who is a manifestation of pure potential, the limiting concept that "you are this." Thus begins the layering of identity.

The layering continues as the toddler is told, "You are a girl, you're a boy, you're big, small, fat, skinny..." "You're weak, strong, smart, dumb, bad, good; you're loved, you're despised." Continually told what he is from birth, he is labeled and taught to identify with *concepts* of who he is: an identity consisting of only a physical form and a false self image, limited to these descriptions.

As children, we begin pretending to try on identities as part of our play. We have been convinced that, to have value, we need to "become" something. Little girls will try on the identity of a nurse or try on the identity of a mommy, using their dolls. Little boys try on the identities of fireman or super hero. In their imaginations, they become these identities to see how they feel, to see if they have become something "worthwhile." Children can take off an identity just as easily as they put it on. They retain the potential to become anything because they do not attach themselves to or completely identify with any of their temporary identities.

Little girls don't "try on" the identity of nurse and then say "I guess that is what I am and what I will always be." They pretend to be one, "play nurse," then take the identity off and once again return to experiencing who they are as an immortal soul, pretending to be a limited mortal.

As children grow older, adults influence their concepts of "what they should be" even more. Adults who do not try to label or teach this limitation, will inevitably program the child anyway, by setting him the example of their own limiting beliefs. The child hears that what he is isn't enough and that he needs to "become something." The need is created in the child to become something of value because he has been convinced that, otherwise, he has no value. Just being God's unique creation is not enough. Can any living entity, such as a tree, have no intrinsic value? Many would value a tree only by how it can serve them. If it provides shade, wood for burning, wood for carving furniture, then it is valuable. So, children are taught that just "being" the one-of-a-kind creation they are has no value, they must "become something."

The child's belief in his own inadequacy becomes the motivation to take on more identity concepts, in order to become something of value. He starts to believe what he hears parents and other people say about him. The real cause of his duality is the forgetting of his original state of being: that he was born whole, perfect and a creation of God. As everything God creates, every flower, every tree, is, by definition, perfect, so, the child, at birth, was perfect because it, too, was God's creation. Eventually, man-made creation replaces God's; the child becomes completely formed by the environment, by the adults, by the school, by peers, by television. This layering process continues and the trying on of identities becomes more of a layering of identities. Now, the child believes "I am this body, I am this size, I am this smart/stupid, I am so pretty/ugly." This becomes the limiting part of the child's identity. As the child becomes an adult, the identities layer even thicker because now he believes, "I am a doctor, I am a nurse," etc. Your identity becomes even more engrained and how good you are at that identity is your value. From that grows the competition for who is most valuable and which identity is the most valuable, producing an endless search for the means to someday feel good enough. Buried far beneath all the false layers, the true essence of knowing yourself as a one-of-a-kind creation of God is never felt again.

As that layering process continues through life, the identity changes continually as more and more images are added. The layering becomes thicker and thicker, as it changes from "I am a doctor" to "I am a doctor, wear this nice suit, own this big house and drive this expensive car." All this is added to the core identity belief. The layering actually grows beyond just the physical form and mental concepts. The environment becomes part of the layering because now your self-image grows out into your world. The layering can become enhancing or detrimental, as identification with a car, house, job, and even spouses and children increases. These additional layers are believed to provide either more or less value.

The true spiritual path is identity "disrobing." It requires no effort and is really about just letting go of who you are not. As Yogi Amrit would say, "you don't have to worry about letting go because you can never let go of who you really are, just whom you are not." It is not about "becoming" something more, as many religions teach. It is about un-becoming and disrobing all of these identities; stripping them away to reveal your true essence. Spiritual realization lies in revealing the true Self with which you were born: the spirit, the immortal soul that was in perfect oneness with and connected to God in that moment of birth. As a baby your "beingness" was love. Before you identified with worldly concepts, your identity was your soul and your soul is God and God is love. A baby's "beingness" is love and sweetness and beauty: the true soul, before it has any layers over it to restrict its expression. All babies are beautiful because they are reflections of that perfection in which they were created. When you look at a baby, you see a soul through an unlayered, transparent body. The process of the spiritual path is one of undoing, un-layering. It's not about becoming more spiritual, it's about becoming nothing, becoming less, unveiling who you naturally were at the moment of birth. That's why religion is not required in order to become enlightened. You were enlightened already and need to go back to being who you truly were; that is the path to enlightenment.

The spiritual path is seeking that which we were the moment of birth. This is the original message of Christ. When he said, "you must be born again," he was not speaking symbolically. He was talking about going back to the moment of your birth and re-membering, rejoining your true identity, which had the ultimate value without needing to "do" or "become" anything more.

True Identity
by Megan Wells

The Soul wants union

The ego separateness

The Soul longs for simplicity

The ego hides best in complexity

The Soul wants to be transparent to allow the light to pass thru

The ego wants to hide, distract and deceive
to insure problems and job security

The Soul wants to reveal the magnificence of its Self

The ego contrives images to mask its self

The Soul trusts love and opens to it

The ego feels exposed & wants to run or fight
to protect its hiding place in the dark

The Soul stays connected to share the abundance
it not just possesses but is

The ego creates a distance to try to hold on
to the little it thinks it has

The Soul breathes easily

The ego struggles to get enough
to fill the void it lives in day and night

The Soul is at rest in the arms of the One
who created and loves it forever & ever

The ego builds a fortress to hide behind for what it thinks is
safety only to be locked into battle behind it with its many
warring selves

Chapter 15

Aperture of the Heart

"God and I are on the same page, He wants
my love and I want to give it to Him" - MM

Suddenly, in the midst of a conversation with a close friend, my body froze in stillness and awareness of my heart chakra became totally amplified. The experience began with the feeling of a blazing light of Divine Presence. In the vision, my heart looked like the aperture on a camera; opening and closing, adjusting precisely to the intensity of the light. However, in this case it was adjusting to spiritual light and the adjustment was quite the opposite of a camera lens.

My heart chakra naturally opened wide in a receptive state to receive the light and joy emanating from the presence. Then, just as abruptly, this Divine Presence began to recede into the background and my heart chakra's lens began to close down in response. As God's presence approached me again, the aperture lens of my heart chakra effortlessly opened to be bathed in the blissful light.

Once again, the presence receded and I experienced a sense of separation between God and my awareness; the aperture closed. I was then shown how the distance placed between my awareness and God's presence was in exact proportion to the opening and closing of my heart chakra lens; it literally reflected the distance placed by my consciousness between my self and God. I watched the lens open as I approached God and close as I distanced myself. Of course, I did not want the distance and craved the closer experience of the source of all joy, so, during one of the experiments I used my will power to try to keep my heart lens open despite the increasing distance. Excruciating and unbearable pain in my heart was the result!

From this experiment, it was clear that the intense pain of separation from God closes the human heart so that it feels less. In that state, when the heart is closed, very little of anything can be felt. The feeling apparatus is shut down in a self-preserving mode. Feeling nothing is a way of lessening the pain. The "feeling nothing" reaction does nothing to remove the cause of the emotional pain: feeling distant from the real source of joy, peace and bliss. It is rather a version of the "fight or flight reaction" animal instinct, applied to feelings, a deadening of sensitivity.

Spiritual awareness allows us a glimpse at how an open and receptive heart can be the solution to feeling separate, alone and emotionally starved. Rather than trying to force your heart open with your mind (the concept of "I should have an open heart"), only the self-created separation from God needs to be addressed. Once the desire to feel God's presence is uncovered and allowed to grow, the opening of the heart becomes automatic. When spiritual longing is allowed expression the law of attraction always brings God closer. When the protective instinct of closing down the heart relinquishes itself, it is replaced with the natural urge to receive all that the heart desires: to be bathed in the abundance of God's loving presence.

A flower does not use energy to open; it only uses energy to close up to protect itself. When no force is exerted, it is open. In the same way, an open heart is our natural emotional state. This truth is also reflected in the example of "ease" being our body's natural physical state along with Peace as our natural mood. When all that is of fear is let go of, peace is what remains.

Our hearts and the flowers share the quality of openness and receptivity to the source of light. What we fail to realize is that feeling less pain means we feel less of everything. Feeling less of everything is the basis of spiritual starvation. Spiritual starvation is the cause of all of our problems. Feeling with fullness is what brings contentment and peace.

When we say we "love" something it is really that we are feeling ourselves being fully present and experiencing with all our attention and focus what ever we say we love. This allows us to be filled full (fulfilled) since we are being totally, wholly (holy) receptive. It does not matter what we are doing, it is that we are there experiencing with all we are so all of us lives fully in the experience. If you only partially experience something in life you are only partially fulfilled by it. The part of you that will be fulfilled will be the part of you that has been open and receptive. We all love the feeling of fully experiencing not what we are doing but fully experiencing ourselves in the act. We love experiencing with our whole Self because it is an experience of unity consciousness. That is the feeling that everyone is craving and believing it is found in the object instead of the awareness of our own Self experiencing what we say we love. Different experiences and beings can inspire and trigger our being open and fully present but the experience we feel fulfilled by is that of wholly feeling our Selves.

Chapter 16

Fixing Your Steering Wheel

"We all can manifest perfectly, we just visualize imperfect conditions and manifest them perfectly" - MM

Most people in this world are busy seeking power. They believe that all their problems in life involve not having enough power. Everyone pursues power in a different way. Some people pursue it through money, believing that if they just had enough money it would overcome their feeling of powerlessness. Others believe if they just had enough fame that would eliminate their feeling of powerlessness.

Life really isn't about getting more power. It's about how you use the power you have and if you know how to focus it: the difference between an untrained street fighter and a holder of a black belt in martial arts. The trained fighter has learned to use the energy he has in the most efficient way. It doesn't matter how much horsepower is under the hood of a car, if the steering wheel is faulty. No matter how much power you have, you will only get to the wrong destination faster.

Most people think they need more and more horsepower under the hood (of life) or more and more gas in the tank (resources). This is related to thinking they need more influence in the world and more affluence from the world to make their lives easier. The truth is, it is all about fixing your steering wheel (guidance). Fixing the steering wheel of your life means refining your purpose for being here and refining the direction in which you are heading. It also involves refining your understanding of where you are going and why. To have a successful life, it is more important that you use the power, affluence and influence you have in a more precise and refined way and it is best to fix your steering wheel before you step on the gas.

We all need at least one day a week set aside for introspection (fixing your steering wheel). I suggest a day in solitude in nature to just "be". In silence alone in nature you can take stock of your life, distance yourself from your day to day existence and gain an objective view point to clarify where you are headed and why. This day of rest from the world is vital to healing your body, mind, and soul. It is a necessity in rectifying your direction and prioritizing how you use your time and energy. The simplicity and peace of nature will heal you from the disease of over complexity so prevalent now in our man made world. Over complexity is toxic to our minds. Spending time in simplicity allows detoxification of the mind; a prerequisite for peace.

Chapter 17

Eternity is not Endless Time

"Lead me from the unreal to the real, from darkness to light, and from time-bound consciousness to a timeless state of being" - Yogi Amrit Desai

Is eternity nonstop continuation of endless time; time forever? No, eternity is not an endless supply of time, as most people think. Eternity is actually a place. That place is an "internal" realm that can't be found outside oneself. It is a natural place, one everyone has within, which can be discovered with practice. By meditating and practicing serenity, a one-pointed perception, inwardly focused, slowly arises. This is the direction of spiritual awareness, which can be achieved again and again. Eternity thus becomes a place one can visit with ever-increasing frequency.

Eternity is a place of total stillness, a place of total peace, like the center of a merry-go-round that is spinning. The riders on the very outside of the merry-go-round experience massive movement and change, with gravity's powerful pull outward. This pull is so strong that they must hang on or they will be flung off. Similarly, we can experience physical life as pulling us outward into the world with its ever-increasing gravity of material existence or approach the one-pointedness of the center, where movement is barely perceptible. Being "in the center" is a very different experience from being on the outside.

The center of yourself is where you can find complete stillness, silence and peace, a realm where there is no time. The experience of entering that place of no time is literal: you enter a more awake state than the physical state of day-to-day consciousness. It is as different as the normal waking is from the sleep state, only in the other direction-- more awake.

In the timeless state of being, duration cannot be measured. A second or a million years may have elapsed in an experience of no time. This state is beyond the material world, which is required for measuring time. Time is perceived only in the physical world. It does not exist in the mental realm: you know from your own experience, that if you are having fun and forget to look at a clock, time goes by faster; when you wait in a line, time goes very slowly. Time is thus completely dependent upon your perception.

When Jesus said "I will be with you until the end of time," he meant "I will always be with you in the place of timelessness." In other words, when you transcend beyond time-bound consciousness, Christ's consciousness and His presence is always there. Eternity is a place and not a time.

The end of time, in the Mayan calendar, occurs in 2012 and many believe that time will end then. Actually, in 2012 the human consciousness will have attained a sufficient spiritual level to be able to experience a timeless state of being. Since time only matters if we believe there is a beginning and an end, we can then be identified only with our immortal souls, where time is irrelevant.

Chapter 18

The Truth about Heaven and Hell

"He who gives the most love wins" - MM

What really does happen when we die? I'd heard theories and seen movie scenarios but none really satisfied me. I made a sincere request for God to reveal the truth and, within days, I was shown the answer through example.

When we die, we don't really die; there is merely a transition from one "place" to another. God offers us a greater awareness of Him by giving us a greater awareness of Truth, so when we leave our physical bodies, we get a "Life Review," which is neither a punishment nor a reward. Since the true purpose of living is spiritual growth, our final experience in a lifetime enhances this by giving us even greater awareness.

The Life Review is the experience of your entire lifetime from the perspective of the "receiver," while God remains non-judgmental. In truth, we are one with God and, because God is everywhere and everyone, we too are one with everyone. In the Life Review, we are given this awareness. Separateness is seen as the illusion we had while in our physical bodies.

We are never really disconnected from anyone or anything. Everything that we think, feel and do affects everyone and everything, not just on the earth, but also in the entire universe. It's hard to comprehend that our thoughts, words, deeds and emotions affect not just our own mental, physical, emotional and spiritual bodies. For example, our own physical health affects the health of the planet (the physical body of the Earth), though our individual effect may be small. Our emotions affect everyone's emotions, as part of the emotional body of the Earth (the sum total of everyone's emotions). Likewise, the mental body of the Earth is made up of the sum total of all the thinking minds on the Earth. Not only do we contribute to these larger bodies, but also we receive from them in kind, by means of a "resonance" that connects us with vast storehouses of like vibrations (for more on this subject, see *From Enoch to the Dead Sea Scrolls* by Edmond Szekely).

Because physical form gives us the illusion that we are separate from everyone else, we commit acts that are harmful to "others." We lack the awareness that doing something to someone else also does something to us. The Life Review allows us to re-experience every event in our lives from an expanded awareness. How difficult this is to imagine, with our limited intellect, which lacks the capacity to comprehend the enormity of this process: to actually review every minute of your entire life on all levels. Freedom from the limitation of the physical body allows us the temporary possibility of this vast perspective.

The Life Review is not a "thinking," but actually an "experiencing." You "feel" your life as if it is being done to you. The experience is not a vision; it is rather like trading places with those who were the recipients of all your actions. You are in each of their bodies, experiencing each of your actions as they did.

If this "Life Review" were to show you only the highlights of your life, the people that you impacted and affected the most, the greatest good and the greatest damage, it might be enough to impart awareness. But the Cosmic Law is exact and complete. In the greatest sense, it is Divine Justice. Every beautiful and loving act you bestowed would feel as if it were being done to you. In a sense, it really would be done to you, because you momentarily attain the awareness of the recipient of your kindness. If a hunter could experience what the deer he shot felt as it died, so, this is precisely what the Life Review offers us, on a much vaster scale.

"Do unto others as you would have others do unto you".... is really "do unto others because you are doing unto you. " This explains why, after we leave the body, we experience either Heaven or Hell. We get everything we've given out, back, in its precise method and measure.

Since there is no time beyond the physical realm, the process happens all at once, creating the intense sensations of Heaven or Hell! If you gave love and kindness, you will reap that; if you caused a lot of pain, you will reap that; not for punishment, but to gain awareness.

This is the truest meaning of "What ye sow, so shall ye reap." You experience everything that you did, in your entire lifetime, done back to you. If you helped someone or made someone feel loved, you will feel loved; if you hurt someone, you will feel the hurt as if it were you to whom it had been done. The result of the Life Review is a great awareness of your actions, all the good and all the bad. Hell is the recognition that there is nothing you can do to change that; the agony of awareness, so to speak. The result of the process is the realization that all that I did was not done to anyone but my self, for those who were wise enough to spend their life with a sincere motive to please God the experience is Heaven.

Chapter 19

Two Kingdoms

"Environment is stronger than will" - Yogananda

Picture a kingdom with a ruler who is sympathetic with the needs of his subjects. His subjects, though they are at his mercy, do not live in fear, but rather in safety and peace. They work not only to support themselves and each other, but also happily work together to support the king, because he is a beneficent ruler with their best interest at heart. The king is kind and knows that the object of his leadership and power is not to exploit and control his subjects, but to care for and serve them. He is always open to hearing their concerns and immediately takes positive actions to fulfill their needs, knowing that in doing so all, including him, benefit. He listens with a concerned ear to all their grievances and resolves disharmony immediately to minimize disruption of the peace in the kingdom. He knows that everyone, including himself, prospers to a much greater degree when there is peace and harmony amongst his subjects. He knows that conflict merely wastes energy that could be productively used to benefit the entire kingdom.

Now, picture another kingdom. In this kingdom, the king is selfish and ignorant that his way of ruling not only diminishes real wealth and prosperity of his subjects, but also his own, because he can't, in any real sense, separate himself from them. He uses his absolute power to control his subjects and heartlessly exploits them. He obliges them to work long hours, feeds them poorly, never shows gratitude for what they contribute, never allows them time to get enough rest from their endless duties, nor time to completely heal and replenish themselves. His demand for the work he requires is endless and unreasonable.

On top of all this abuse, his subjects live with the stress of constant fear of his insensitive demands, which, in most cases, will involve actual physical harm to them. Living under these stressful and fearful conditions, the subjects are not at peace with themselves and therefore quarrel with each other in their attempt to merely survive. Their communication with each other comes from desperate survival needs and is always strained. One part of the kingdom fights over extremely limited resources and food with other parts of the kingdom. The conflict and fighting drains the subjects of the little energy remaining to them from living under this type of ruler. When requests are made to the king, he rarely gives what is requested, but instead attempts to pacify the subject with more of something that is not needed or requested. When subjects are forced by emergency to tell the king of some disharmony, the king has them drugged to silence them with the excuse that he is keeping the peace and addressing the subjects' pain. The king never addresses the cause of the pain because he thinks that is too much trouble and will require too much change. The conditions in his kingdom of unrest and disharmony increase with each passing day and revolt by his subjects is imminent.

The kingdom in these stories is your physical body. The subjects are the cells of your body. You would never consciously choose to live in a kingdom at war but you may be doing just that. What kind of king are you when it comes to ruling over the kingdom of your own body?

Your real environment is your own body. If your body is not at "ease" if it is suffering from dis-"ease" you do not live in a peaceful environment for your mental and spiritual health.

For more guidance on this subject see <u>Don't Pollute Your Own Stream</u> AKA <u>You're Not Fat You're Swollen</u> by the same author

Chapter 20

A Whole Breath is a Holy Breath

"It takes One to know One" - MM

Everyone understands that constrictions to the flow of blood cause circulation problems and strain the heart (blood pump). The heart then must exert more energy to move the blood through the obstructions. Most people are not aware that the same is true for the lungs (air pumps), although we all know that if we completely sealed our skin with paint, we could suffocate because our skin actually breathes.

Even less understood is the truth that we not only breathe with our lungs, but our entire body. The body expands and contracts with each breath. Stiffness and lack of motion in any body part inhibits us from taking a whole and satisfying breath.

The number one <u>nutrient</u> required by the body is oxygen (yes, oxygen is a nutrient). Most people are starving for it because they can't ever take a full breath. We can live without food for weeks, without water for days. But, we can't live without air for more than a few minutes. We consume 2,500 gallons of air every day. It is air, not food that gives us 80% of our energy. Because it is our greatest nutritional requirement, many of our appetites are symptoms of starving for air. Many diseases, such as cancer, only thrive in an oxygen-starved body.

Our bodies are so flexible as children, that we can breathe fully and effortlessly. Much of the joy children feel emanates from the cells of their own body. The first experiences of fear cause babies and children to begin to hold tightly to their bodies. Before then, they are naturally relaxed. All tightness in the body is caused by the mind's holding on. It is commonly believed that the body itself is tight, but this is not true. Once the life force and mind leave the body at death, and before the onset of rigor mortis, the body is instantly limp and completely flexible.

Imagine spending energy concentrating on trying to hold your nose on your face. This is an obvious waste of energy, no different from holding on to any other part of your body which results in holding it tight. Think about the amount of energy that would be freed up for more creative activities if not wasted in this unconscious way. Perceived threats to the body cause the mind to cling to it and sometimes even hold it closed to protect it. Long after the threat has passed, the body/mind forgets to let go.

We all understand that anything that lets us breathe easier is a relief. There is a corresponding pattern for each state of mind. Fear changes our breathing pattern, as do all emotions. Breathing is tied to our thoughts and, as thoughts affect breathing, so does breathing affect thoughts and thought affects consciousness. Being able to take a whole breath is not only healing to the body but also expanding to the consciousness that is tied to the body. Ultimately, a whole breath is a holy breath. A whole breath is only possible when all fear locked and stored in the body has been released. Learning how to let go of the unconscious habit of holding the body tight is extremely healing.

The most efficient method of attaining the healing of letting go is thru properly practiced hatha yoga.

Whole Breath Yoga is a technique discovered by the author thru 40 years of practicing yoga. For more information see Whole Breath Yoga by the same author.

Chapter 21

Keeping God Company
Our Ultimate Purpose

"To "do" or "be" that is the real question" - MM

One day I began to question what it really means to serve God. I had just heard about someone who made a great contribution to feeding the hungry and I felt I had done nothing of that magnitude. So I asked God if He wanted me to take up some righteous cause in the world and was surprised at His answer. He told me that many people are doing things for God and few are "being" with Him. He explained that He is the ultimate "doer" and can "do" anything He wants. What is lacking is having someone to keep Him company! He said "Doing is creating and I am <u>THE</u> Creator.

I created humans to keep me company and to share My creation with Me." He explained that He has everything but companionship.

He pointed out that man, instead of sharing the creation, became enamored with it and forgot all about Him.

This would be like wanting to spend time with a friend you love and deciding to go to the county fair together. It was something you planned to do together and being together was the primary motivation of the plan. Once there, the fair is so interesting you forget you went there to see and share it <u>with</u> your friend. If fact, you become so involved with what's going on at the fair that you forget about your friend completely. You become disconnected and loose contact with your friend altogether; lost in the fair. This is how we are with God. The world is the fair and He is our truest friend.

God pointed out that the time I spend alone in nature, just "being" with Him is more valuable to Him than anything I could <u>do</u>.

Being with God, in communion, allows you to share in His Presence, which allows you to "be" His Presence in the world. When it comes to serving others, is there anything the world needs more than God's Presence?

This is still one of the Discounter's (see previous chapter) favorite digs: to try and convince me that being in communion with God is not as important as something else. The "doing frenzy" continues in our culture and, unfortunately, churches today do not stress that time alone, just being with God, is a priority. Even church activities draw the attention to the external world, when God can be found more readily within. God pointed out that if the twenty hours a week that people spend in church activities were spent in silent meditation and communion with Him, man would become enlightened in a relatively short time.

He also showed me that being in our true place with Him, we would be *creating* with Him. It would not be "doing" anything as we normally think of creating: more like being a channel for His Divine Energy. In that way, He would be creating through us. Everything created this way is new and original, unlike what is created out of doing, which is merely man's re-arranging what has already been created by God.

He showed me an example of what it would look like when this type of co-creating is actually taking place. I can only describe it as similar to watching time-lapse nature films, where you can see flowers blooming and grass growing, only it was that energy pouring through my being and creating new life. This is the true meaning of co-creating with God.

In the state of communion with God, there is no desire. Being with God is all full "filling". You can't possibly feel want. Your only desire, if you felt anything remotely resembling desire, would be to add to the abundance by creating more beauty and goodness, to pour out the overflowing of your soul.

The simplicity of contentment becomes appreciation of the very life in your veins and that life within your body begins to feel like God's presence. Eckhart Tolle was teaching how to feel the life in your own body. He had students close their eyes and, without any motion, try to feel the life in their hands. He asked, "How do you know your hand is alive?" Everyone can feel the life in their hands if they but concentrate on feeling it. In the same way, you can begin to feel the life in your body. When you can truly feel the life in your body and realize that it is the presence of God, it will feel like bliss sustaining you. Each breath becomes an exchange of love between you and your entire environment. You are breathing air out of God's nostrils that He is breathing into you.

He created each of us as a unique way to share His creation. No one can fill the empty spot in God which we are created to occupy except us. He is un-full"filled" until we are back in our rightful place with Him. He showed me this sentiment on the beach one day when I found a beautiful piece of polished beach glass. It had an unusual shape and the artfully sculpted edges looked deliberately designed. God told me to stick it into the moist compacted sand and then pull it out. He asked if there were anything else in the entire universe which would fit precisely back into the impression it had left. He pointed out that only what had come out of that mold could fit perfectly back into it and that this is the way it is between Him and us. No one else but us can fill the void in God's heart which we created when we separated from Him.

Chapter 22

Magnify the Lord

"God's solutions always solve multiple problems with one act. Man's solutions always create multiple problems" - MM

As I study the flowers and plants at my meditation place, the flowers teach me. They explain that although they reflect God's presence, humans are created to do something even more special. Nature only reflects God's presence but humans can magnify it. This is why we have been given a separate will; not so we could go against God but so by our free choice we can add our little will to His and magnify it. We were created to magnify the same way a magnifying glass does with the sun's rays or an amplifier does with sound vibrations. We can magnify to a greater power the presence of God. This is not really changing or distorting it, only increasing the intensity. The quality of magnified sunlight does not really change in its makeup or affect other than to do what it does in a more powerful way. The amplifier of sound does not alter the notes of the music, it just increases its intensity and effect on the environment and on those waiting to hear or receive the music. In this same way we were created, unique amongst all creation, to increase the presence of God by adding our will to His. It is like God is voting for doing things his way and we second the motion.

Our separate will is our greatest contribution or our greatest damage and detriment to ourselves and the rest of creation. When we get behind God's will, which is always an expression of love, healing, harmony, righteousness, light, illumination of truth and justice, we increase these qualities both in ourselves and the world. This is why right behavior/right action is the first step on the spiritual path. If you are out of harmony with God in your behavior, you are not yet even on the spiritual path. You are on some other path, knowingly or unknowingly, going somewhere else. The Ten Commandments and the Yama Niyamas of Yoga express this prerequisite. The Essene teachings explain that before you can commune with heavenly, divine, angelic forces, you must avoid going against Gods will in your behavior or in other words you must master the "thou shalt nots."

"I pray that love and devotion burn like a fire in my heart consuming in its heat the petty, the trivial, the unworthy, and the selfish".

Gyanamata One of Yogananada's earliest disciples

Chapter 23

Talking Flowers

"The only thing that sets man above animals is his responsibility to care for the rest of nature." - MM

One morning I sat down and noticed that only some of the flowers at my meditation place were open. Although the sun was shining on them some remained closed. As I pondered the reason for this, they answered me. "You believe that it takes effort for us to open. This is because you hold this false belief about yourself. This erroneous thought is common amongst humans. We are naturally open and need only to make an effort to close. We do this to protect ourselves from various things in our environment. This is the only act that requires effort. Since being open is our natural state without exerting influence or energy we would remain open."

This news was shocking. I had to admit that I did believe that it took flowers effort to open. I could see the truth that this projection came from a deep-seated belief in a condition of my own unfoldment. I held the belief that being closed is natural and open takes effort. This false idea makes "letting go" frightening since religion teaches us that we must expend effort to be open and that we must fight our very nature to do it. It is true that if we have not yet entered the depth of ourselves, our surface and more limited disconnected aspects may drive our spirit nature off the cliff of endless desire; but in contact with our Soul, our true Self, letting go and allowing ourselves to just be who we are would effortlessly put us into Divine communion; that is, put us into union with our true Self or Soul.

Letting go of trying to be what we already are would bring immeasurable amounts of peace into our lives. We should all just allow our true spiritual nature to express without the self judgment that we should be a different kind of flower or a different color flower so to speak. Trying to be what we are not only distorts us; like a purple flower trying to be white. We are the only expression of God that exists the way we are, so we may as well stop comparing and just bloom.

Note*   If you do not believe that the rest of nature is communicating with us read the Secret Life of Plants by Peter Tompkins or Messages from Water by Masaru Emoto. In the Autobiography of a Yogi Paramahansa Yogananda talks about an Indian scientist named Jagadish Bose that invented instruments that could measure responses from metals and even rocks! Bose says "The telltale charts of my crescograph are evidence for the most skeptical that plants have a sensitive nervous system and a varied emotional life. Love, hate, joy, fear, pleasure, pain, excitability, stupor and countless other appropriate responses to stimuli are as universal in plants as animals". "A universal reaction seemed to bring metal, plant, and animal under a common law. They all exhibited essentially the same phenomena of fatigue and depression with possibilities of recovery and of exaltation as well as the permanent unresponsiveness associated with death."

Chapter 24

Singing With the Birds

"Be ye perfect, even as your father in heaven is perfect" - Jesus

I have often pondered what the rest of nature thinks of us. We are so clumsy that we can not even walk through the corridors of our own life without damaging everything. The sounds, rather noises, we make are harsh when compared to the song of a bird or roar of the ocean, even if it is a rough sea. Even in the destructive storms of nature, life is created and supported, but the noises from man commonly bring destruction to himself and all that surrounds him. His "noises" are almost always at the expense of the rest of life. In the book Messages from Water by Masaru Emoto, some of man's music actually shatters the structure of perfect water crystals.

Try listening to a bird sing when a helicopter is passing over head. There is a clash not a harmony. Ever notice that when two different kinds of birds sing they don't clash or a bird singing and the sound of rain form a harmonious sound? Though they appear to be coming from different sources they don't conflict because they come from the same source. There is the clue as to why we clash. Man is like a mighty baby misusing powerful tools mostly as weapons against himself, others and the environment (which he does not realize is his own greater physical body)

The rest of nature is waiting for this baby to grow into a spiritually mature adult. The rest of nature is waiting for humans to rejoin the harmony of song- to learn to sing on key, to sing with the birds instead of disrupting their song, to live "with" life instead of disrupting it.

To learn any song one needs to begin by listening. Before even listening, one needs to realize that he is off key and does not know how to harmonize with the song that is already being sung. In this case, it is the song being sung by the rest of nature. Humans need to develop the ability to listen not just with their limited ears, but with their entire being. They need to develop the ability to listen with all of their senses, to develop receptivity. It takes humility to know one doesn't know.

First we need to change the egotistical opinion that the purpose of the rest of creation is only for our use. We need to become aware that the rest of nature is aware; is awareness. Generally speaking we are the ones unaware of the Presence in the rest of creation. If all of creation is alive and aware of us then we are the only part of creation unaware of the intelligence emanating from the rest of creation. Does that really make us the most intelligent as we arrogantly believe? We have the potential to be that, but for most there is a long way to go to manifest it.

We can all begin awakening by sitting in stillness in nature and asking to become sensitive enough to experience the communication and communion possible. The Essene's taught communions with the angels of air, water, earth, and light which heightened this sensitivity and awareness. Man may be religious without the connection with nature, but he is not truly spiritual until he reconnects with the holy scripture of nature and learns from it. By careful listening and the desire to be harmonious with nature's song, man can take his rightful place in the choir of life.

Chapter 25

What We Get Is What We See

"Never use your higher Self for a lower purpose" - MM

In this vision I was shown a street that was lined on either side with opposites. On one side were magnificent, beautiful flowers of every color, size and fragrance. The other side of the street was lined with garbage, rotting and decaying things. I walked down this street looking at and smelling every flower. I did not have time to look at anything else because the flowers were so beautiful. At the end of the street I was asked how my walk down the street was. "It was beautiful and I was uplifted", I replied.

I was then shown another person walking down the same street but they looked at the other side of the street. At the end of their walk they were asked how the walk down this street was for them. "It was horrible, ugly, disgusting and disturbing" they replied. Then the voice pointed out that we had both walked down the same street but our experience was completely colored by what we choose to focus our attention on. Both positive goodness and negative ugly were available to us both. I just simply focused my attention on the positive and the other person focused their attention on the negative. Since in the world of duality opposites are always present, it becomes our choice what we perceive out of all the choices. (From a more advanced view point good and bad, likes and dislikes are originated and colored by our own desires)

Many believing they are "realists" play the "Devils Advocate" and focus on the dark side (literally). Why would any one want to be an advocate for the devil? We focus our attention, which is our energy, on what we have chosen. What we water with our attention grows. Magnifying the negative is just that; empowering and adding our life force to the negative. Since both sides are always present we have the ability to respond and "response-ability" to consciously choose where we direct our life force in the form of our attention and thereby magnify and increase whatever we focus on.

When you turn a light on in a room there is no battle; the dark is simply replaced by the light filling the void. Gratitude is a powerful spiritual medicine. It is a powerful antidote for those chronically focusing on lack, what is "apparently" missing, negating what is there.

I listened to an audio course entitled Conscious Language by Robert Tennyson Stevens. In this course he points out that the English language is based on a tremendous amount of negation. Using words like this is "not" vs. this "is". He gave a list of words pointing out they are the most conscious ones to use.

Here is the list:

I can, I am, I will, I choose, I have, I love, I create, I enjoy.

His course was truly eye opening. He pointed out that one American Indian tribe did not even have a word for *"then"* since they lived so much in the present moment.

"Pour what's right into your life and what's wrong will be crowded out." Or in other words "resist not evil."

Chapter 26

"Chosen One."

"Most of our problems are just symptoms of spiritual starvation" - MM

I posed the question to God; *"Do you Love me?"* and received the answer in the form of the following vision: From a somewhat distant and elevated place I saw an endless sea of people. They were standing close together so I could only see their heads and shoulders. They were all looking at each other which did not look in any way out of the ordinary. Then I saw one person who was looking upward into a shaft of light that was pouring down on to them.

As I studied this vision of the solitary person looking up, my vision focused in closer and to my shock I saw my own face in deep rapture looking into the light that was streaming down upon me. Then I heard a voice proclaim *"One choosing ...Chosen one...How could I not hold you dear to me? When you choose me I choose you and anyone can at any time choose me. But it is rare and when they do we meet instantly because I am all the time choosing my children they just rarely choose me back."*

From this vision I got a glimpse of why I am truly valued by my beloved God for most of mankind is looking to each other for the love they are craving when He is right there wanting all the time to answer this need. Almost all that look to each other to be "full" "filled" because they are in a "disconnected from source" state of consciousness, usually have nothing to give that is of any lasting value.

It is the story of two empty cups looking to each other to be filled. In this dance (and sometimes fight) for fulfillment, many hearts are broken and disillusioned because they are looking for love in all the wrong places. This disillusionment is God's merciful attempt to get us to look up.

For more on this subject see authors book <u>IN–TO-ME-SEE</u> (INTIMACY) A yogic perspective on relationships

Gratitude

❖ I give thanks for the mentoring by my spiritually-inspired grandmother, whose example tethered my life toward God and truth.

❖ I give thanks for the awareness of the presence of Jesus Christ and for His guiding me to the greatest teacher about His true nature, Paramahansa Yogananda.

❖ I give thanks for the priceless teachings and guidance of Paramahansa Yogananda (Self Realization Fellowship -originally called the Church of All Religions), who's love has transformed me.

❖ I give thanks to Yogi Amrit Desai (original founder of Kripalu Yoga, now Amrit Yoga), who physically embodied the truths taught to me by Yogananda about Christ's true nature.

The gifts from these sources have been immeasurable
and my salvation.

About the Author

Megan Wells (MegaMom)

The author grew up on an organic farm in Tillamook, Oregon in the 50's and 60's. She was mentored, during her childhood, by a spiritually advanced grandmother. The truths revealed to her in Nature brought her to the path of Natural Hygiene, fasting and the Essene Teachings (original Christianity) at the early age of fifteen. She embraced the teachings of Paramahansa Yogananda (Self Realization Fellowship) at sixteen and began seriously practicing the eight limbs of Yoga (the science of self mastery) as a way of life.

Her forty years of experience and understanding of yoga and spiritual principals has been distilled down to their essence here. The guidance in this book comes to you through the gift of wisdom and the motivation of compassion.

Megan lives on Maui and has one daughter and two grandchildren.

More Gratitude

Thanks to Paramahansa Yogananda for your brilliant inspiration and guidance in the writing of this book

Thanks to Amrit Desai for the title of this book

Thanks to Will for being my greatest supporter

Thanks to Betiana for being my loyal spiritual daughter

Thanks to Nadine Newlight for polishing until it shone

Thanks to Amanda for transcribing sound into sentence

Deep gratitude to Michele and Muhammad Behleem for their spiritually healing music and promotion of my work (starlightharmonymusic.com)

Thanks to Teri Mister for her finishing touches.

(transformationaltruth.com)

Thank you God for blessing me with the gift to hear You

LaVergne, TN USA
09 November 2010

204198LV00001B/47/P